Inherent

Lucía Orellana Damacela

First published 2020 by Fly on the Wall Press
Published in the UK by
Fly on the Wall Press
56 High Lea Rd
New Mills
Derbyshire
SK22 3DP

www.flyonthewallpoetry.co.uk

ISBN: 978-1-913211-29-5
Copyright Lucía Orellana Damacela © 2020

Acknowledgments

Warm thanks to the editors of the publications in which the following
poems first appeared, sometimes in different versions.

Anapest: "Grinding"; Automatic Pilot: "Embroidered Past"; A Restricted
View from Under the Hedge: "Satellite"; Dash: "Altitude" and "Mango
River"; Duende: "The Páramo Train"; erbacce: "Lemon"; Eye Flash
Poetry: "The Inside Tree"; Helen Magazine: "Ink Carved Rusty Path"
(Winner of the First Visual Prompt Quarterly Contest); In the Name of
the Voice: "From the Deck"; Mulberry Fork Review: "Bare View"; One
Sentence Poems: "Joy, Repeat"; Orbis Journal: "Rain Noir"; The Peeking
Cat: "Before Monday" and Young Ravens Literary Journal: "Beached
Moments".

Contents

Beached Moments

She runs on a Pacific beach
    by her mother's side
    hair braided with sunshine and salt.

She tiptoes in the ocean
    open   enfolding   relentless
    the smell of future.

She looks for intact seashells
    jarred in her room
    in the pint-sized apartment
    shared with a roommate
    she barely knows.

She looks for round pebbles
    bedrocks to her cacti
    in the window sill of said apartment
    where the brick wall from the neighbouring building
    blocks most of the sunlight.

She looks back
    happiness is colours and shapes
    bursting in her hands.

She searches for her mother's gaze.
That gaze, she couldn't keep.

The Measures of Time

Diving of albatross seizing on slippery rockfish.
Waiting of lion by the river.
Yawning of zoo-confined grey wolf.

The cuckoo clock startling Christmas at Abuela's.
A fitness band making judgments on the running journey.
A woman freeze-framed tai chi motions in the park.
Jamming of cars, sweat and summer swears.

Five minutes' walk between home and school
multiplied by twelve years minus two minutes per journey
for four glorious months, until somebody stole the blue bike.

Grinding

They become alive in the kitchen, those wheat flour
particles that didn't make it into the oven as dough

for our breakfast bread, and float around with the sunlight.
Dressed in black from head to toe, Abuela walks through

the beams and dissolves the vision. She grinds coffee
with a heavy Universal mill iron-clamped to the table,

turns the crank holding it from the wooden handle.
With every turn she crushes the coffee beans further

until the crank has no more resistance from inside
the funnel and the beans have been all reduced

to powder, releasing an aroma as familiar as the 7 a.m. news
on the black and white TV. I want to turn the crank,

and she, as always, gives me a swift *No*, still turning
the crank, the pot with boiling water already on the stove.

Ill for a while, Abuelo died at the hospital two days ago.
He wanted to be cremated, his ashes released into the

ocean, sailor until the end. I heard Mom and Dad
pleading for his wish. Abuela gave them a swift *No*,

that's not the proper way. And she keeps grinding
the portion for today's coffee, right before we go

to the funeral home. The coffee there, she says, is terrible.

The Páramo Train

The Andes. I have seen them from above,
running on loneliness and shivers.
They go on forever. The páramo, the passing place
on the way from the city by the estuary to the city by the sky.

When Dad was alive and I was twelve, La Nariz del Diablo.
I imagined a rollercoaster ride where coins would fall
from our pockets,
and the Cóndor would eat from my hands the offering I brought,
my wonderment.

The cool mountain wind squeezes out tears like rain falling
horizontally,
like a bullet train, like the drops of a limón stomped by the boot
of the hacienda's owner on his way to collect the tribute
from the peasants, a few generations ago.

I wish the train would ride straight ahead, but no hope. It goes
up and up, snake climbing in concertina moves. The train
charges forward while I go back in time. In the same railroad,
una niña travelled to the highlands with her father. The father
visited a yesteryear friend; la niña met the friend's son.
They played cards until the light bulbs started blinking at them,
and she felt like a grown up for the first time.

The mountains, all that Sol, king, god, Inti crashing on
stained-glass windows. We are visiting Dad's hometown
church, just like we did before. The light, emboldened,
interviews the Stations. This, our Via Dolorosa.

Heading with Dad to the snowy slopes. The Sun looks at us
from the side now. Our best side. The blue above is the blue
of truth, splashed with purple and orange and red, raw scrambled
eggs of divine birds, ancestors of the Cóndor.

This rarified air invites you to become one with the land.
Dad's ashes are snowed under now.

Knife Sharpener

The whistle call
precedes his shadow
on the evaporating road.

Straw hat between the sun and him
the sharpener wheel protruding
from the cart top and its rattling noise

Every fifty or so steps he hawks
Afilo cuchillos Afilo cuchillos
tobacco-infused voice a blunt tool itself

A pair of scissors and two cleavers emerge
from a yellow house
with gardenias and black iron fences

He whirlwinds the air
blades infuriating the incandescent sun
the rattle now a steady buzz

Abuela waits for him
every Wednesday morning
with dull edges and cold horchata.

Break In

She breaks into abandoned houses;
leaves her shoes on just in case,
despite having lived in countries
where you don't do that;
brings sandwiches and a drink
to these fabrics of decrepitude;
spider webs, the thinnest of walls;
mechanical clocks still working;
books waiting to be touched again,
tamed and then forgotten pets
she rehomes.
Each house her Everest, her English Channel,
the heights and lengths she conquests,
the stage where she becomes indomitable,
splurges in old smells and words.
A low-burn rumble inside.

Abuela's Superpower

She eye-measured things with such precision
she knew at once where she could store them:
a sliced giant watermelon, no problem,
she had the right fit container.
A stew leftover, ditto,
as if the leftovers were left
based on the exact size of the available bowls.
The flowers from her garden,
here, she brought the perfect bunch for the vase.
Our childhood pictures,
her photo album had enough room for each one of us.
Love, betrayal, pain, losses, illnesses, deaths,
she, the velvet-hands vessel took them all.

Mango River

going through a narrow passage, struggling
to keep the canoe off the bank, we grab
mangoes from laden trees dangling over
the river – flavoured suns in our hands – eat
them taking no prisoners, fling the naked pits
in the water, make them perform for us, dance
in mid-air before splashing. These slippery,
furry, fake golden coins, skipping once, two,
three times; we fill their hollow skins with
water and squeeze them hard; watch their
amber juice flow back into the river, liquid
sunset. Light receding behind us, we paddle
upstream, fast, as pits and skins drift away,
flimsy marks of our last day of summer.

Abuela's Garden

Her hand-knit sweater clads
the early morning of the tropic.
Back bent, hair tied in a bun, uneven steps.
Smells and textures her garden Braille;
the wisdom of her hands the main fertilizer.

She still ventured outside her house,
to the iglesia, to the tienda,
before she became invisible,
withered away, a whiff of the essence
once stemmed from her locks,
a whisper of her song.

They inhabited her; roses, geraniums,
and wildflowers whose names scape.
Birds and insects carried them away,
expanding her shrinking world.

The Window

Numbness in her legs,
she flower-gardens her universe.

Unfaithful witches
that flee as soon as she
falls in love with their
shimmering pageants.

Like the gardener
with an oversized razor
who leaves behind an aftershave smell
of freshly-cut grass.

The wind
—that voyeur,
undressing trees at will—
touches her and blows her hair no more.

The rain
—a truthful visitor—
saturates her core, unyielding whip
branding her bones.

All she has fits in here,
this window and this front porch
which the sun reaches
before burying its head in the far ground.

The evening's thunder
sends her down a wormhole of memories
from where she returns with the scent
and exact burgundy of her childhood peonies.

And a blossoming wish.
These grounds are not yet receiving
her biodegradable, ultimate present.

Vacant land beyond the fence,
she hereby exists.

Altitude

As she mountains
        breathing falters
the scape from this snowed-shell lies
behind the curtains where she and her sister used to hide
at holiday parties
but there are no chats now
only numbing silence
lulling the snowfall
that interrupted
roads and plans.

She eats a paltry ration
        crackers and chocolate
in hibernation mode
being high doesn't fit her   this altitude
      I mean   *don't you see it?*
      Me either
Was her infant crib this cold?
She must be misremembering.

As she falters
        breathing mountains
        she only sees the curtains, white.

P(l)ain

Things hidden by shine,
foliage
wiped out by afternoon glare.
Barbeque at parents'
out-scheduled by random encounters.

When being yourself
—forget the yourself, just being—
involved high heels, low voices,
pain on ice
with salt and lemon.

Wooden stakes pointing at you,
skewers holding meat chunks,
not yet seared.

Mourning

Funeral at thirty-six degrees,
the music weights more,
heavier, also, the smell
of exhaustion squeezed
out of armpits encased in black;
a cotton-woven grief cast.
Candles fade,
lilies decay,
quiet talking blossoms.
We address each other's despair
with soft words and embraces.
Voices come to a halt
when Rafi, the old lab
lying next to the coffin,
moans as if he is the only
living being on the planet.
My mind goose bumps
with the realization that Rafi
is beginning to grasp
that no treats or cuddles
will be offered to him again
by those crossed hands.

Embroidered Past

I still miss not seeing you
at your finca anymore,
sheltering under your porch
from a sun as tropical as your fruit compotes
and your plantain delights.
You, who once told me that a woman
is not a woman if she doesn't know
how to make cheese, which I don't,
but I could find out.

That was
before your speech
became harder
for me to understand.
Before you spent
most of your evenings by your window,
reading the Bible until the day
had extinguished its last light.
But then you had the light in you,
you believed.

Now I have, by way of my mom,
the embroidered linen your mother made,
your mother whom I never met except in the altar
you kept across the main living room window
with pictures of her, your dad,
and your first-born son.

Seaside

My likeness   splashing fragments
a disgruntled puzzle

My hands   a leaking carrier
unsuitable to scoop broken mirrors

A reflection

no more   an impulse perhaps
the jump of the gull squawking
to the shadow of a minnow fish

A call

a wail without a colony to return to
an empty claim
a face without an image

A thought

the calm after the wave
short-lived deception
until the inescapable fluid
that lies below the surface
takes hold   a reverse birth

A gist

underneath
what my feet feel   no more.

Hairlines

Day suits me. Lights on me, I am alive.
A blotchy colour work, the sunset
doesn't cover all the greys in the sky,
which makes for a messy photo finish;
underexposed   the twilight
anonymizes trees, blurs the edges
of the hills and the houses.
Road and mailboxes
hybridise their shape.

I retrieve the always found wanting mail
and try to figure out
how not to disappear in the aftermath of light.

Toast

Light doesn't touch me at this angle,
melted torch of dimming thoughts
which boiled in the kettle a tad too long,
before I serve tea on your white china.
The tea set has held its own against the pull of time;
a ricochet to mindful crochet sunsets you enjoyed
before becoming the ghost of your own place.

A sumptuous piece of cake
is not served to celebrate that I have changed
the texture of the minutes I embroider
in this story; that I am moving far away;
but then, the sunset.
We swallow it up
like a passion fruit/strawberry/raspberry jam
thinly spread over a pumpernickel toast.

It Is

like wheat crackers for tigers

like soya drinks for sharks

for this blind and unabashed hunger
kernels of faint love cannot satiate.

Sand Burial

What remains of a boat
      rotten wooden body
      rusty metal frame
beachgrass tying it up
to the sand.
Condemned to decay.
Whiff of ocean voyages
still with it.

Trapped like me.
      A sea of expectations
      anchored me
      as if buried in dark matter
      heaviness held my body
      seawater saturated the sand
      intensified its lead
      its smell   its coldness.

But I found the power
to lift my legs
stretch my arms
and walk away.

When I looked back
the water had already
evened the surface.

Satellite

My mask collection remains in my hometown
boxed in the utility room of a building
with fish-bone antennas.
The mask I now wear is pale and winterized.

The piranhas that hunt in my bloodstream
bite with fluency of familiar griefs
leaving a feeling which could be fear,
but slightly more complicated, involving grit.

Keepsakes preserved with camphor balls.
Diminutive moons. Moon is also the cold mirror
to look inside my mouth at the doctor's office
when the lump in my throat becomes unbearable.

And the old building got a facelift and now has a satellite dish.

Mementos

Containers, receptacles for things
to be preserved, counted, treasured.
Stored instants, receded surprises,
topics in lethargy, an Acheron crossed,
Nirvana of the minutia, the eternet of things,
dated, undated, object memory.
Frontispieces, beheaded presents
on the tabernacle of time.
Scents with decanted appeal.
Nothing like the smell of camphor
to abhor perdurability and the idea
that holding stale things ransom
equals to owning the moment.

Bare View

An operating room sets tent in front of my apartment.
Surgeons perform with oversize machinery to remove rocks
like tumours from an open body.

The offending growth, a fine building eviscerated from the
ground where a giant tower will take its place.

Looking at the now bare space, I long for the afternoon shadow
on the garden where I walk my dog.

It still amazes me, when I think of it, how that sky tickling
structure was torn down so swiftly
in session after session of controlled destruction.

Razed from the land, erased from the memories; gone for less than a month,
I can barely picture it.

My friend lived on the twelfth floor; we could see my dining
room from her kitchen window. An out-of-home experience,
to observe my things without me around.

She didn't have to endure the fall of her former quarters.
Never left the operating room where surgeons attempted to
remove tumours like rocks from her open body.

Lemon

A perfectly good morning gone to waste
a lemon that kept rolling and couldn't
stop being sour
        a slightly greener sun.

Wanted this morning to be
as delicate as
a net to catch
the last of the butterflies
that still visit the Mexican flame vine
and the summer beauties
that I planted when
there were still many
butterflies around.

The sunlight penetrates my pores
like dust sifting through the net
like wings escaping my garden.

Lemons had a purpose last night.
They made salt look glamorous
and lightened up the Margaritas
        Mexican flames at night
        Things looking less close
        to extinction then, than now.

How to make it all go away
from my forehead.

Sun Love

Summon the sun
into a glass container
drink the summer
with clinking hope.

Brew some lemon tea
lie down with lover
lick each other's
salty promises.

Prepare some limoncello
with the mouth-
watering memory
of a honeyed moon.

Melt a lime candy
under the sun's tongue
hyphenate kisses
interlock shadows.

Grab the sunset by its colours
—drips from an orgasmic orange
wipe it from mouths
preserve the thirst.

Drenched

Happiness wears a hospital gown,
pours colostrum like a jubilant fountain.
Our new-born a concave dream on my chest.
His smell of honeyed grass
his hair the soft blow of the most ancestral force
the echo of stars aligning
to render everything in the universe
bright and perfect.

Sleep Over

The moon and the stars crash on my floor
through the open window
at the end of one of those days
that seems to have sucked up
all the energy of the world.
I let them rest.

Something Borrowed

I always thought
I have my mother's eyebrows.
Now that I have a daughter,
I see she has my mother's eyebrows.

I don't have my mother's eyebrows;
I am just passing them along.

The Limits to My Love of Nature

The wasp
that stung daughter,
my green thumb crushed it;
and then I crushed
ice to lower the swelling
on her face.

Before Monday

Sunday stretches like a cat.

At noon, seasoning time.
Simmering recipes conjure up
aromas
drift and escape through open windows;
invisible trail brings back
the bikes and the kids
who don't know
these smells come
really from Abuela's kitchen.
Yearnings for home,
released.

Later in the woods
when the sun is low and amber,
dressed in copper, the trunks of trees
escort our walk, drenched in
that goodbye sort of light.

Building Blocks

He is a teenager now, but the sight of a boxed
challenge makes his eyes twinkle just as much
as when his charmed child fingers shaped and
reshaped stations and buildings, monsters and
robots, ships and airships. Again Again Again.

Holiday

As the doorbell rings,
wonder shimmers the gifts
nesting under the tree.
The frigid air gets in first
but their presence melts it away.
She tries to reach the tree-topper
and falls short.
I lift her;
she smells like apples;
we giggle,
she brushes the star,
I doff
the sparkles of glitter
from her little hand.

Joy, Repeat

Jubilant Sisyph,
the neighbourhood kids climb and go down in their sleds,
carving with their laughs the snowy hill.

Housekeeping

Silence,
starched and folded in a dresser drawer
next to a sachet of cedar shavings
to keep it prim.

Fear,
crushed in the recycling bin.

Loneliness,
permafrosted on the ice cream.

Anxiety,
off the bathroom cabinets;
stuck to the bottom of the hiking shoes.

Indulgence,
bookmarked on page 57
of the Ecuadorian recipes' book.

Strength,
crammed inside the bed springs,
pushing up the morning.

The Small Bang

Its shape shifts
thanks to my pneumatic help
from a lethargic piece of rubber
to a yellow fully-rounded form.
Its perky lightness makes us
gravitate toward it,
minuscule reachable sun.

But you don't know
when to stop, do you?
Stressing the cheery surface
to its limits, all is left
is the lingering rebuttal.
A sunshine promise
now reduced to its empty core.

Intruders

In the MRI, ambers float randomly
inside a clear bag.

In my uterus, heartless pulsating heat,
kicks and punches.

They talk to me in burning bursts,
feed and expand off the oxygen in my blood.

They argue *we are benign,*
don't mind us, we are a happy family.

Your mother had us too, do you remember?
You are so much like her, inside and out.

It must have felt different, I tell myself,
carrying them from carrying me.

They have shrunk to silence now,
but they still rumble in my head.

The Inside Tree

No grass around the path
to the beach; only dry weeds
that tickle the morning's thirst.

A gaunt tree stands
alone amidst the arid shore,
its roots down my throat.

Once, I almost choked
eating a cherry while driving.
Swerved down the road, red and airless.

Wisdom—or luck—is to stop,
pull all the strength you can muster
to cough it out or pass it through.

Once, I lived by the sea,
my lungs devoured the clear air,
weeds and sand tickled my soles.

Rain Noir

An air-sucking candle by the window sheds the only light
while the thousand knives of rain
slice the world into shreds of grey
which memory sews back together.

The road a gigantic aqueduct
downstreams a mixture of sky water
and disgorges from the insides of town.

Without asking permission or forgiveness,
water stains the back fence,
the shed's wall and leaky roof,
the air, the night's silver.

Outside warped by a screen of disfigured sounds
and crashing images, nature's Rorschach,
shuddering with the ghosts
who find their way home amidst the thunder.

What is it about rain which unburies fears and regrets
left to rot next to the garden hose?
Opaque puddles along the formerly even ground
wait for the dark to set its trap.

After rain, the essence of everything
which has a stake at life.
Freshly-crushed grass and tilled soil.
The smell of second chances and redemption.

From the Deck

Rubbers screech by the adjacent road;
the creek courses east on the other end.
Greenery above us stencils the sky
into a puzzle of light
seemingly at peace with itself.

The dog's onyx shadow
bolts towards the neighbours' back yard
in pursuit of wild game.
Used to chases, rabbit takes its pointy ears
elsewhere.

Dog returns to our garden
victoriously holding next-door dog's
stuffy animal,
similar enough to the rabbit
to be a proxy bounty.

I seize some fresh air, mute river and road,
return the stolen good, unsure, for an instant,
about whether this poised blue sky
and this purposeful green mesh
are the proxy or the rabbit.

Ink-Carved Rusty Path

Blue bike consumed by rust
at the bend in the trail,
leans on notched,
scratched, skinned tree trunk,
which, instead of shutting down,
sprouts from its open wound;
healing power of chlorophyll
or anything that believes in relentlessness,
like the wooden book exchange
stand by the road.

Leaves left there are hand-bound,
bleed freshly written ink,
set forth a journey
from seaside to mountains,
to landscapes of words unknown,
with oxygen that gives life
and oxygen that corrodes
in every stroke.

About the Author

Lucía Orellana Damacela is the author of *Longevity River* (Plan B Press, 2019), Sea of Rocks (Unsolicited Press, 2018), and *Life Lines* (The Bitchin' Kitsch, 2018). Lucía's work has been published in more than twelve countries in both English and Spanish, in venues such as *Tin House Online, Carve Magazine, PANK, Fly on the Wall,* and *The Acentos Review*. Born and raised in Guayaquil, Ecuador, Lucía holds a PhD in Social Psychology from Loyola University Chicago, tweets at @lucyda, and blogs at notesfromlucia.wordpress.com. She currently lives in Connecticut.

About Fly on the Wall Press

A publisher with a conscience.
Publishing high quality anthologies on pressing issues,
chapbooks and poetry products, from exceptional poets around the globe.
Founded in 2018 by founding editor, Isabelle Kenyon.

Other publications:

Please Hear What I'm Not Saying (Anthology, profits to Mind.)
Persona Non Grata (Anthology, profits to Shelter and Crisis Aid UK.)
Bad Mommy/Stay Mommy by Elisabeth Horan (May 2019. Chapbook.)
The Woman With An Owl Tattoo by Anne Walsh Donnelly
(May 2019. Chapbook.)
the sea refuses no river by Bethany Rivers (June 2019. Chapbook.)
White Light, White Peak by Simon Corble (July 2019. Artist's Book.)
Second Life by Karl Tearney (July 2019. Full collection)
The Dogs of Humanity by Colin Dardis (August 2019. Chapbook.)
Small Press Publishing: The Dos and Don'ts by Isabelle Kenyon
Alcoholic Betty by Elisabeth Horan (February 2020. Chapbook.)
Awakening by Sam Love (March 2020. Chapbook.)
Grenade Genie by Tom McColl (April 2020. Full Collection.)
House of Weeds by Amy Kean and Jack Wallington
(May 2020. Full collection.)
No Home In This World by Kevin Crowe (June 2020. Short Stories.)
How To Make Curry Goat by Louise McStravick
(July 2020. Full Collection.)
The Goddess of Macau by Graeme Hall (August 2020. Short Stories.)
The Prettyboys of Gangster Town by Martin Grey
(September 2020. Chapbook.)

Social Media:

@fly_press (Twitter) @flyonthewall_poetry (Instagram)
@flyonthewallpoetry (Facebook) www.flyonthewallpoetry.co.uk